A Coloring Book
Walking for Clean Water
Pukatawagan on the Move

EE-PIMO-TAN-NEWA TA-PEE-KA NI-PEH

PAKEE-TA-HAW-GAN YE-MECHEE-TELE CHILC

JANICE SETO

Translated into Cree by RALPH CARIBOU

A Coloring Book: Walking for Water - Pukatawagan on the Move

ISBN: 978-1-926935-42-3 (printed)

DEDICATION

Anita Yasuda, the writer, my friend, my inspiration
Mrs (Ada) Johnston
Ann Celli
Mom

- Janice Seto

To my wife, Loretta, my children and grandchildren

My parents and grandparents for passing on the
knowledge of the Cree language

- Ralph Caribou

Janice Seto (Cree translation by Ralph Caribou)

Pukatawagan
(copyright 2017 by Janice Seto)

CONTENTS

ACKNOWLEDGMENTS
Ku-man-mis-com-mechilc

The members of the Mathias Columb Cree Nation (MCCN) in Pukatawagan who marched on the 1994 Journey for Life – and our supporters from MCCN and other First Nations along the way.

The Community Economic Development diploma program of the University College of the North – executive, staff, and above all, the students

- Ralph Caribou

Huge thanks to illustrator, Ekasaputra!
Three more words: Ekosi, Ralph Caribou!
- Janice Seto

Ka-ki-thaw Mathias Colomb ne-he-thaw-wak Pakits-ta hawk-kanik Ka-ke pe-moo-tee-chilc ee-kos-pee 1994

Pemotee who-win who-chee aka men aka-he-we-chee aka ana mena kakewechee ka pawistak kowak kak heko tee who chic Mathias Colomb Cree Nation akaw mina kotakak athasin thewak

Anima Community Economic Development diploma netewhochee University College of the North – one kanee wak, okiskin nawahamakewak, mawatchee ekiskenohamacik

A Coloring Book

Walking for Clean Water

Pukatawagan on the Move

Ee-pimo-tan-newa Ta-pee-ka Ni-peh

Pakee-Ta-haw-gan ye-mechee-tele

CHILC

Janice Seto (Cree translation by Ralph Caribou)

Mimi was sleeping when something woke her up. What is that strange sound? She tiptoed in the dark, careful not to wake her puppy, Maskwa, and opened the door a little.

She saw her Daddy weeping.

Mimi kenepaw kekawthin kawaspaw wehekot, kekawn anima ithekow ke ma yak kotakaw?

Nesikatak kasip pweeteet tepiskanook, heka tawas paweehat ocheemis-sisak, Maskwa, apisees kapas-kiteena yesk quateem.

Awapamatt opapawa hewachoo ye thit

Grandmother was leading prayers in Cree and in English for Mimi's older brother. He was ill, and getting worse. His skin had these vivid rashes and he could not eat without pain. Her mother even used traditional medicine for his healing.

Kokw keyammeha hewew he-ne-etho-weet aka ehaka thasimote Mimi ochee osteega. Hehakoosit aka awasimeek eeatee he-ha-ko-sit.

He opeegua sakeepatheet aka heka he-kee meechesoot. Oh mamawa ahpo innetha-too maskeekey ch-petchee tat ta me-thoyat.

Three days later, he was feeling better. The family was grateful her brother was jumping up and about in his bed ready for Halloween.

Then Grandmother got sick.

Nestoo keseeka yespee, keymethomachee noo. Kakeethoo kananeskomowak osteesa equa quas kothee thit nepewineek asa emaneet awe cheepa ekeesikathik.

Kokuminaw aha ateehakosit.

There is something wrong with the
water, the doctors later told Mimi's
mother.

Nantow oma yeespatik nepi,
maskeke ethinew keeheetew Mimi
ohmamawa.

Mimi tried to understand. Her home was close to the lake and she walked with her friends there after school. "The lake looks clean to me. See, there are lots of pike fish."

Mimi kekaquew misquew thetaw.

Wekewak, kegewak sakahekanik kakehastethik aka yekota kepimotew mena whechewakana apone sokoolewit. "Yee kanawapata methowasin wethow owma nepi, yee, mecheet kinoosewak."

The next day after class, Mimi and her chums and Maskwa checked out the Missinippi River. "The river looks clean to me. See, there are lots of pickerel fish."

Mimi and her family and friends live in northern Manitoba, in Pukatawagan, which is the Cree language word for 'place of many fishes.'

Ke tom yekesikak, Mimi aka wecheewakana aka maskwa natawapenikewak Missinippi seepee. Methosin wethoma neepi, yee, meecheet okawak.

Mimi aka wechisana aka wecheewakana Ahaychik kewetinook, Pakitahawkanek, hetea kameecheechechik kenosewak.

8

Finally, Mimi asked her mother, "Where is the bad water from?"

Father replied, "From the tap."

Shocked, Mimi blurted, "The bad water is <u>inside</u> the house?"

"It is inside every house and every building, Mimi. Even your school."

Peethesk, Mimi akaklosew chimatl, umamawa, tantee ooma whoche, kamachakamik?

Opapawa heyetikoot, "Kapemapochekeyak."

Hesachipathit, Mimi ahetweet, "Petookamik na ahochipathik owma nepi?"

"Kakethon waskahekana, Mimi, Kiskimohamake wekamik mena."

"And Mimi," added Mother, "Do not play in the water near the water treatment plant. You could get sick."

Mimi's eyes went round, "My friends play in the smelly mud there! I must tell them!"
She ran out of the house to warn her friends.

Mimi, ki-tikook umamawa, Katha metawee kesewak nepi mina owta whopani. Kake hakosin.

Mimi, metunnee mamookechapew, necheewakanak metaweak yekoota asiskee! Pooko ta wetamawakwak.
Ah wathowepatat tantee wetamawat wecheewakana.

Walking back home after Christmas church services, Mimi asked her Grandmother, "When can we stop boiling water?"

"Our Chief and Council say we must boil a little bit longer. We are waiting for the government to fix the water plant."

Yepakeewechik yepone ayamiha newuntik, Mimi aka kiwchimat Oh-kuma, tanspi kaponee oseena now nepi-eh?

Onekanewak eytweewak keyapick kineskew-sk. Kepehanow okimawowin tahusitat.

Mimi sees more people in Pukatawagan getting sick. Older people and her school chums of the Mathias Colomb Cree Nation cannot get up from their beds.

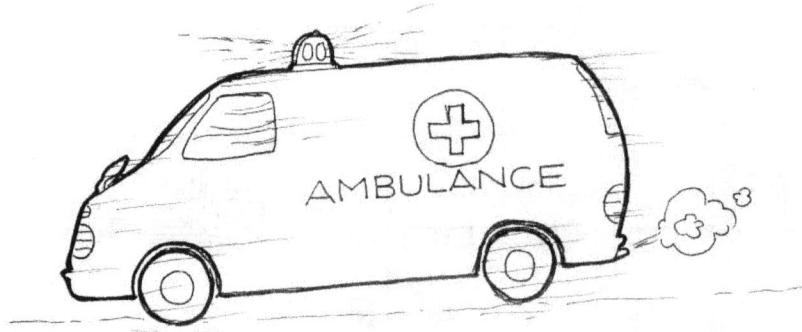

Mini wapamin awasime micheet yeatee hakosithit. Kisee-aya aka owe-cheeschothawakana, mowach keehatee waneskathewa.

On June 29, 1994, the chief medical officer of Manitoba, Dr. John Guilfoyle, declared sewage was contaminating the water in Pukatawagan.

"That is true, the water is still brown with floating junk," the people told the Chief and Band Council.

Opinaywipism neso-kekach-metahat yetake-mhet 1994, aw-okimaska ontahohe hewin Dr John Guilfoyle, akeychee etweet, mo-ach meth-thosim nepi Pakitahekanek.

Tapwee, keya-pitch mecha-kamin aka yeyakootee kequan, ethinkeewak kitachik ow-nekaneewa

In July, Chief and Council leadership decided to evacuate Pukatawagan. Anyone who could travel got out by plane and train to The Pas where the water is clean.

Opaskowipisim yetakim-mht, onekaneewak kesekimewak kakethow awethewa tanekataquak Pakitahawkan. Kakethow wawinak kakaskitat tapimowteehot keyposew otapanee opasquoia-esi yetee eypeka nepi.

The Opaskiyak Cree Nation opened their
hearts and homes to host Mimi's friends and
family. Bannock is shared, along with stories.
Mimi loves homemade jam on bannock.

And still they waited for someone from the
government to fix the water plant.

Opasquia ethinkewak kepasketeeen-namok
wekewawa ta kepisihachik Mimi aka
wecheewakana.

Kehapitch kapehochik okimawiwina
tahositathit nepi.

15

The women of Pukatawagan then wanted everyone to walk along the major highway all the way to the government legislature. "We want everyone to know we are walking for clean water. This is our Journey for Life," said Mimi to Muskwa while putting on her running shoes.

Eako ehtawin Pakitahawgan ketaswiwak tapimotechik Maskawa mesakawi eskochi kichi waskahekunik. Kakethawawina netatawithewawan yepimoti-ak tapeka niphi. Yehko uma yipimo-otihowa pimatisiwin hochi

The newspapers wrote about this peaceful walk to Winnipeg for clean water.

The federal government minister reads about the Journey for Life and sees it on the tv news. He travels to meet chief Ralph and band council members of Pukatawagan and other First Nations leaders . Even Elijah Harper, their federal Member of Parliament, got an invitation.

Achimo masina-ek-kawa ke-achimowak kapimotani-wa tapi-ka niphi. Okimawowin ah-yimitaw, yepimo-tihowa pimatisiwin-ohchi akwa mina wahpatam eychekastittinthik.

They met for many hours in the teepee at the Opaskyak Cree Nation near The Pas.

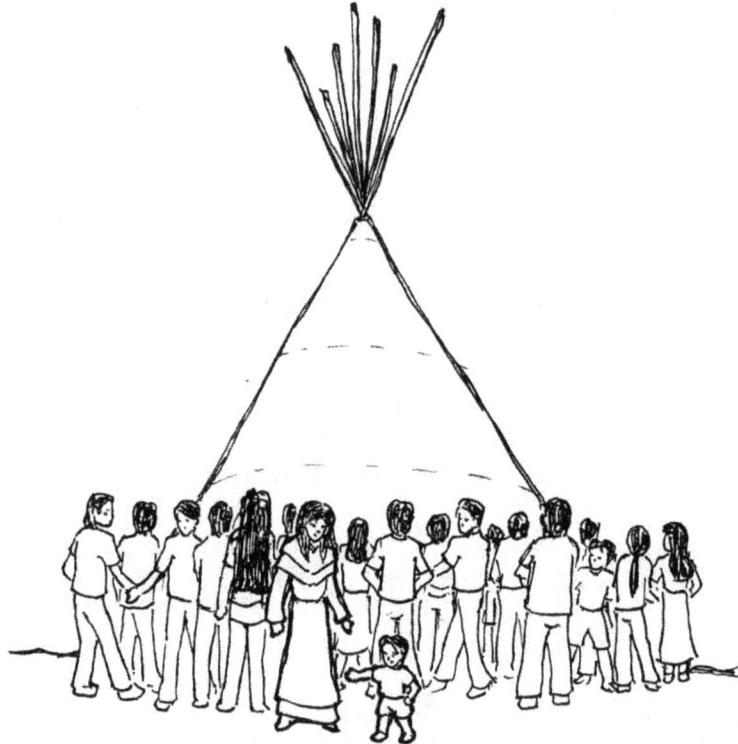

Pese-powehotehw ey-pe nakisakawat okimakana Ralph akwa othaso-sowe ethiniwa akwa ownikanewa. Apuo Elijah Harper, Ottawa ka-pekiss-kwe-stamamik.

Kin-wesk kanakis-kaf-tochik meke-wahpi yi-cotee Opasquia.

Mimi and her puppy, Maskwa, and her family and her friends and over 200 of their family members and band chief and council members from Pukatawagan walk on the Journey for Life to fix the water plant. Everyone takes turns to carry the banner of the Mathias Colomb Cree Nation.

Mimi akwa kochimesisa Maskwa, akwa wechisana akwa wichiwakana aki awasimi neso kichi mitanow kawakomitowchik kepimoteewak eako anima yepimo-otihowa pimatisiwin hochi. Kaekethon-awina mamikoch kepimotataw Mathias Colomb Cree Nation pimaschichikan.

19

Along Highways #10 and #6, cars and buses honk their horns in support. Many First Nations Cree and Ojibway-Cree gave them food and places to stay at night on the 800 km journey. Shouts of encouragement keep everyone's spirits up when it rained and when the sun got too fierce and when people's feet got tired.

Mesakami ye-ako meskanow # Metata, otapanask-quak ke-tepwimohewak wech-kapawistawachik. Micheet methiwak kipaki-tinasowak michiwin akwa kapi-siwin. Sekiskatowin kakithow-awinak wechi-hik tee-kimiwa mina ohsam kate-kisasteek, aka ate-wisakisitesi-quak.

The federal government agrees in writing to build a new water treatment plant in Pukatawagan. Mimi and everyone else would now have clean water to drink and wash in!

Okima-owin tepa-kethimow oska-ye taho-sitat oh-tawhopan. Mimi akwa kakithow awin-nak ta-pican-thew niphi ta-wini-kwechik.

21

The Assembly of First Nations looks at all the other reserves in Canada and sees that many other places have bad water too. They want all the peoples to have clean water too.

I-tee okimakanak kakistapichk kanawapetamok kakethow iskonikana we-stawow onipimiow eka eh-methosini thik. Natawithitamok kakethon ithiniwak who-niphimiwaw ta-petkan-thik.

This became the Green Plan for all
First Nations reserve territories in
Canada.

Ke-atitastew woma, aski
othanowewin, kakethow-ochi
eskonikawa.

Mimi hugged Maskwa delightedly, "See, your tired Pukatawagan paws walking for two weeks helped every First Nation band."

Mimi akash-kitinew Maskwa yemoochikitheta, kewapateen, ethiko ka-cha-ki-in kisi-ti neso yees-pathe epimoti-in kakithow wawinak kiwichi-how.

At home in Pukatawagan, Mimi goes
netting fish in the winter and spends her
summers on the land. Peaceful and quiet
days of canoeing along the Missinippi
River, gathering medicinal herbs, and
camping with her family and Maskwa.

Ispi- eta-kosi Pakitahawgani, Mimi
neti pakitahw ipiponithik aka nipinthik
papami-ayaw, yi-papamisak Missinippi
Sipi, yemanahoot maskiki-ak, ekotawit
kis-sik wechi-sanak aka Maskwa.

Mimi graduated from high school and college, drinking clean water from the tap - like every other Canadian.

Mimi kepostatotinahow metakat mina ayespakewanthik, mine-quew ye-peganthik ni-phi-pe-akan kekethow awinak uta Canada

26

NOTES FROM THE AUTHOR

The Journey for Life, the organized march for water by Pukatawagan's Mathias Colomb Cree Nation to the Manitoba legislature in 1994, did indeed happen. The provincial chief medical officer for health did declare a boil-water alert on June 29, 1994. The water treatment plant did eventually get addressed, albeit after a long delay.

There was extensive coverage in the media at the time of these events. Unfortunately, the Journey for Life occurred pre-electronic communications technology and pre-digital social media and thus this significant event of 1994 in Canadian First Nations political action stayed in the grey shadows. It is hoped that this children's book restores Pukatawagan in the country's narrative.

Ralph Caribou provided the translation of this story (by Janice Seto) into the Cree language, specifically the Rock Cree dialect. He welcomes queries for further information on the Mathias Colomb Cree Nation and Pukatawagan, where the water is now safe to drink.

###

ABOUT THE AUTHOR

Janice Seto writes non-fiction and commentary including articles for The Bridge, the publication of The Malaysia-Canada Business Council.

Her published books include a two-book series on her late father - *Johnny's Place: The Coronation Restaurant in Bowmanville* and *Johnny Seto's Bowmanville – An Enneagram Perspective.*. Her more recent books are also available on Amazon: *Standing Out in The Background – A Guide to Extra Work in Toronto's Film & TV Industry*. She co-authored *The Expat Teacher Job Search Guide* with James Rogers.

Bowmanville's Octagon House – From Church and Faith and Tait to Irwin & Seto went to #1 on the Amazon Bestseller list free download in its category during Easter 2017.

Walking for Water – Pukatawagan on the Move, translated into Cree by Ralph Caribou, is her first children's book.

http://janiceseto.wix.com/words
amazon.com/author/janiceseto

ABOUT THE TRANSLATOR

Ralph Caribou comes from a long line of storytellers in the Swampy Cree tradition and culture. A community-spirited man, he has served the members of the Mathias Colomb Cree Nation of northern Manitoba, Canada in several capacities, including terms as Chief and over 30 years on band council. Ralph and his wife, Loretta, a certified teacher, and their family continue to make their home in Pukatawagan.

www.ingramcontent.com/pod-product-compliance
Lightning Source LLC
Chambersburg PA
CBHW081234020426

42331CB00012B/3164